Dzogchen Compassion

Keith Dowman

Dzogchen Now!
Books
2012

Dzogchen Now! Books
www.keith.dowman@gmail.com

ISBN: 9798453410828

Font set in Times New Roman 10.5

Contents

Introduction

Compassion is the one single word that encompasses the entire meaning of Dzogchen. Is it more pertinent than *rigpa*? Undoubtedly rigpa describes the exclusive nondual cognitive aspect of Dzogchen, but such abstraction fails to provide any heartfelt meaning. Add an adjective to the notion of compassion – 'great compassion' – 'superlative compassion' – and the matchless nature of Dzogchen compassion is better expressed. Its nondual nature, its innate, transcendental nature, is the nature of mind, the awareness that suffuses the spaciousness in which the totality of all our experience is contained. Its greatness is what sets Dzogchen and all nondual reality apart. Recognition and identity with it in the here and now render all affective emotion pure and simple and its ultimate cognitive aspect supreme. Great compassion infuses every Dzogchen moment. It is the nature of the infinite variety of bodhisattvic expression that permeates the six realms. The nature of our mind realized, no state of mind lacks great compassion.

The word 'compassion' in common English parlance refers to an empathetic feeling for another human being or living creature, literally 'fellow-feeling', 'feeling for another'. Somewhere between 'pity' and 'empathy', it is a passive yet high and vital quality akin to love (*agape*). Such is its formal meaning. In Buddhism and Hinduism, the Sanskrit word *karuna,* one of the most evocative words in that language, rules as the highest expression of affective mind-states. In Tibetan it is '*tujé*' (*thugs rje*), and in the vernacular attaching *che* (great) to *tujé, tujeche* is the common word for 'thankyou', literally 'great-heart'. In mahayana Buddhism this mutual Tibetan sentiment describes the pinnacle of human identity or achievement in the verbal form '*tujechenpo*', ('*tujechembo*', '*mahakarunika*', 'great compassion'). In the Mahayana it is universally venerated, and worshipped – particularly among the common people – as Chenrezik, 'He/she-who-gazes-with-tearful-eyes'. In Vajrayana, Chenrezik becomes the yidam Tujechenpo, 'he who with a thousand arms and eyes serves all sentient beings until the end of time' (see below, *The Birth of Tujechenpo* p.59).

The English language is short on synonyms of compassion. 'Love' is the large, common, word that encompasses all shades of its meaning, whereas 'compassion' itself primarily communicates selfless love (see *Christian Charity and Compassion*, p.61). As in an alternative rendering of *karuna* in Tibetan, *nyingje,* the accent is on the pity that a responsive heart feels for the distress of another.

This relative compassion that manifests in a temporal, dualistic world is enwreathed in harmony and peace and is associated with one of the variable levels of joy. In the timeless realm of Dzogchen where 'compassion' is 'great compassion', to the satisfaction of all, it is the joy, *ananda,* that is called no-joy on the fourth level of joy.

In the Dzogchen view the great compassion of Vajrayana is known as the pristine awareness that suffuses and illuminates every moment of consciousness. Thus pristine awareness in itself contains an ultimate love that has neither subjective nor objective referent. It is a love that cannot be initiated or cultivated because it is already present, fully mature. This all-suffusing, all-encompassing, overarching, natural presence is intrinsic to every moment of awareness.

Insofar as awareness is pristine and compassion is great in its transcendence, Dzogchen is a unity of compassion and awareness. Once the sense of self that strives for its own self-serving interest has abandoned its devilish thrust, dissolving into itself, the natural empathetic awareness that is revealed is called compassion or great compassion.

Insofar as nondual awareness embraces all perception, indiscriminately, nothing is omitted from its compassionate purview.

The awareness is the compassion and the compassion is the awareness. In the first case awareness subsumes compassion while in the second case compassion – great compassion – includes the awareness, which then has an all-embracing cognitive function. In the Dzogchen view there is never anything but compassion. Nothing exists but compassion. Compassion is the whole story.

***

In this Dzogchen view, in this nondual compassion, no distinction is made between the passive compassion that *feels* an all-inclusive oneness in the universe, showing itself perhaps in mystical revelation, and the active compassion that shows itself in altruism, where kindness is as much working towards the fulfilment of universal purpose as disinterested and selfless physical activity for the benefit of others. This distinction between passive and active compassion, which may be restated as the distinction between potential compassion and realized compassion, is anathema in Dzogchen. In Dzogchen there is no gap between the conception and the act, between moral cause and effect, only the spontaneous awareness of a timeless moment of perfect relevance to unitary self and other, unitary microcosm and macrocosm. An identity with the nature of mind is as much compassion as active intervention as passive force. Each timeless moment is comprised of unitary being and doing, and whatsoever that may be it is an inevitable harmony of totality.

If we may speak of compassion as a *feeling*, it is a sense of harmony in totality, and in the identity of 'being' and 'doing' there is a radical sense of completion. Thereby we can arrive at a definition of compassion as 'whatever sustains the complex universe as "completion" while simultaneously sustaining the integrity of the person as pristine awareness.

Compassion is thus the integrity of existence and activity that is sustained for the continued survival of the planet, of the universe, of *being* totality. We can understand compassion as the one word that comprehends reality in its entirety, the one single notion that like the flower upraised by Mahakasyapa Buddha expresses the entirety of Dzogchen.

Compassion at once overrides every pattern and every suggestion of doctrine. Compassion at once embraces all human beings whether they are open to it or not. In this context we remember that Dzogchen is all-inclusive, although beings may not be aware of that inclusion and despite any rejection. Dzogchen subsumes every religious category whatsoever, although religion may not be aware of it or appreciate it. Dzogchen is the ground out of which all religions arise. No religion exists that is not subsumed or transcended by Dzogchen. Dzogchen is the very nature of mind in which all thought has its origin and its existence. Nothing can be conceived that is not rooted in the nature of mind and the nature of mind is compassion.

Compassion can also be expressed as *bodhichitta*, 'mindstuff', the 'enlightened mind'.

To establish the meaning of this overriding compassion through negative definition, this great Dzogchen compassion is not a sentiment arising in an 'I' with an inherent empathetic feeling for others. This compassion has no seat nor object of focus. It cannot be attained by anyone. It cannot be possessed by anyone – there is no-one to attain or possess it. With any sense of personal identity this compassion is lost. The discursive thought that concep- tualizes self and other as separate and distinct and insists upon a dislocation of inside and outside, and 'ne'er the twain shall meet', expresses an absence of this compassion.

The alienation inherent in a sense of personal identity disallows compassionate awareness.

The expression of compassion in negative terms must immediately be punctuated by an assertion of its inclusivity. Insofar as it is the nature of mind that arises in and as awareness, nothing whatsoever is excluded from its purview. If karma presents what is an apparent anomaly, a moment in which an element of conscious perception appears to be excluded from the whole, immediately, inevitably, spontaneously, it is realized as an integral part of the totality. In this way pristine awareness (*ye shes*) creates an inclusion of karma as pure presence (*rig pa*). Compassion may thus be considered as a Dzogchen meme, or perhaps *the* Dzogchen meme. It incorporates nondual reality in a single notion and reproduces itself prolifically in space/time in whatever cultural milieu it finds itself.

It would be a fault to believe that Dzogchen holds the Good as the greatest benefit of the greatest number. Such a belief is an opportunistic fallacy. The Good is for the benefit of all, otherwise it is more of the same ole bad. The spontaneous expression that is Dzogchen is simultaneously for self and other; in a nondual world where self and other are one there can be no alternative. Where the Dzogchen bodhisattva enacts selfless service to demonstrate the process of karmic purification for beings struggling to overcome inert karmic impediments, Dzogchen incorporates the view illustrated in the Buddha's Jataka stories, tales of Sakyamuni's past-lives. Here the bodhisattva acts selflessly for others without counting the cost, although the naivety of the form of this scripture is replaced by a view that encompasses the totality in timelessness.

***

Insofar as great compassion is all-embracing, it cannot be defined in the dualistic manner of 'empathy for another'. Insofar as it is unitary it cannot be defined by a split into dualistic self and other, subject and object, creator and creation. Nonduality and the tropes by which it is characterized are anthropomorphically symbolized by the adibuddha, which in the Dzogchen cosmology is illustrated as *Kuntuzangpo, the all-good.*

We do not need an anthropomorphic symbol to evoke compassion or the nature of compassion, or the unitary awareness of being and doing that is *rigpa*. Indeed, the graphic two-dimensional or plastic three-dimensional representation may prove to be a red herring. Even to provide it with a name may reduce its existential potency. We can wonder why and at what point in human evolution we felt the need to objectify the inconceivable here and now. Why did we need to bind in name and form what was and still is beyond our power to replicate? It is as if human beings were on the verge of losing their identity with the divine and required a mnemonic aid firstly to sustain it and then later to return to it. Whatever the cause, the name for that divine nondual reality that was about to go out of fashion was named Kuntuzangpo by the Tibetans, Samantabhadra by the Hindus, names that can be translated as the All-Good, in English. Such were appellations of the adibuddha, the original or supra-buddha. We need go no further than that name to evoke the compassion that lies at the heart of nondual reality. The reality that Kuntuzangpo personifies tells us the entire story.

We may accept that the move to represent The Incomprehensible, The Inscrutable, in a graphic form indicates a downward trend in evolution, but it's what we've got and may prove a life-saver to people hovering on the brink of what Kuntuzangpo represents. His/her androgynous form designates the nondual awareness that unites passive and active compassion, the nondual experience in the timeless moment of pure presence (*rigpa*), the presence that is inseparable from and only accessible in ordinary consciousness. This anthropomorphic symbol embodying Kuntuzangpo, representing awareness of great compassion, is a naked blue buddha form. Leaning towards the Buddhist tantric tradition, this all-embracing singularity of experience in the here and now, this anthropomorphic form, Kuntuzangpo, represents two-in-oneness, the union of male and female.

As the All-Good Kuntuzangpo, compassion is the singular all-inclusive nondual reality of experience of the here and now. But equally totality is expressed by each of the 100 wrathful and peaceful deities. Looking with the critical eye of intellect this multiplicity of symbolic buddha-mind may appear as a broken, partial, reflection of the whole. But in existential nondual reality it appears always and only an unbroken singularity; each of the 100 wrathful and peaceful deities personifies a complete and total descriptive statement of the nature of mind. Likewise, all the deities of the entire Buddhist pantheon are artistic representations of the multitudinous ways in which the nature of mind expresses itself to sustain the universal integrity that fulfils the bodhisattva vow.

A vajrayana literalist may argue that traditional iconography makes a distinction between the deities of the pantheon that show the 'third eye' – the iconographical representation that indicates an intrinsic awareness of nonduality – and the deities that lack that third eye. Such an absence indicates the loss of the crucial identity with the pure awareness that is the empty nature of mind. But such a distinction is purely academic. The Dzogchen view incorporates all experience into an enlightened mandala where everything conceivable, every thought or image, partakes of the enlightened mind.

***

'Dzogchen compassion' is a description of a nondual existential state of being. This introduction has attempted to clarify that most difficult concept, but how can the ultimacy of the here and now be described? It is impossible; any attempt is absurd. It can however be indicated by allusion and although such allusion may sometimes appear facile if not downright nonsensical, the danger of ignoring the great compassion, overlooking the nature of the timeless here and now, leaving us caught irredeemably on the horns of dilemma, a duality without recourse, is the sad existential hiatus of our rationalist, pragmatic lifetime. This focus on the ultimate view, on great compassion, covers only a few pages, whereas the relative, subordinate, parts, take up the remainder of the book, and the space provided here for description of those relative manifestations of compassion, relative compassion, as *karuna,* belies the overriding importance of the ultimate view, the great compassion.

To say it again, Dzogchen compassion is ultimate compassion, all embracing, free of any moral or emotional constraint. Such compassion, *tujéche* in Tibetan, can be understood as the essence and totality of Dzogchen, the totality of buddha, the entire story of nonmeditation. Compassion is the abstract concept 'nonduality' expressed in emotive human terms, adding poignancy to what is formless and without characteristic. Such compassion, like Dzogchen itself, transcends description, defies representation, and can be resistant to poetic allusion. The peaceful and wrathful deities may appear to have relative meaning and substantial affect, but they are but mere illusion, reflections of the nature of mind, an apparent something evolving out of nothing.

But why then is the overwhelming amount of space in this primer devoted to an exposition of mahayana compassion? It is not that through the relative application the absolute is known, although that may be true, but because the mahayana ethos is the most effective lubricant of the bodhichitta that awakens us to the Dzogchen view. Although any form of action of body, speech or mind, socially moral or immoral, can arise in the timeless moment of Dzogchen experience as the only expedient, relevant and fitting, in that moment, fulfilling the bodhisattva vow, nevertheless the weight of application rests with the good and wholesome that is laid down in the Mahayana. To say it another way, the Dzogchen is forever identified with nature of mind, which is impartial and disinterested, has no preference for good over bad, and remains locked in an automatic, imperative demand for totality-fulfilment. The ultimate no-joy forever arising in the nature of mind – regardless of any contrary judgemental thought arising in dualistic mind – is the feeling-tone of the here and now and which is always redolent of the blissful transcendental sense of moral fulfilment.

***

To continue the excuse for the heavily-weighted mahayana component of this text, given that there is nothing finally that we can do to induce rigpa and its great compassion, and accepting that no amount of hinayana self-discipline, mahayana morality or vajrayana skilful means will have any crucial effect, why should we concern ourselves with bodhisattvic altruism or tantric transformation? Nothing that we can do will make any decisive difference, nothing at all, definitely not, let us be clear about that. However, once we have an intuition of the nature of mind, once we have caught even a slight glimmer of mind's nature percolating through the mire of karmic self-interest, it behoves us to magnify the action-patterns associated with such revelations and which are yet perceived darkly through that glass. Without accepting the dualistic motivations of Buddhist or Christian do-gooders, 'those naïve idealists who support philanthropic or humanitarian causes or reforms' or the facile justification of Baden Powel's boy-scouts, for example, nevertheless we accept that the bodhisattva vow is the natural expression of the nature of mind realized. Likewise, the do-s and don't-s of the prophet Moses and Sakyamuni Buddha (notwith-standing the indications that have an irrelevant cultural origin) are useful expressions of that light of the mind and therefore not only dispel any incompatible pall or create new conceptual barriers but actually open the way...

Wrathful and Peaceful

The wrathful and peaceful deities represent forms of compassionate awareness experienced in the nondual here and now. As such we should know them as symbolical forms of great compassion and they may be recognized as such by whomsoever they may benefit. Evoked, named and descriptively sketched here, primarily, we have the opportunity in vajrayana time, to revel in the pure pleasure that great compassion induces. There is no better expression of the bodhisattva vow than spontaneous indulgence in pure pleasure shared with all sentient beings, and in the spontaneous revelation of any of these hundred compassionate aspects of mind's nature the Dzogchen view is consummated.

But, secondly, we need to know how compassion shows itself as skilful means in the infinite variety of bodhisattvic activity. Certainly all we need to know is Kuntuzangpo, Samantabhadra, and that is all we ever know in the here and now, but to fall into the ignorant belief that everything is always relatively peaceful and serene is to deny the ultimate transcendent nonduality of every possible moment of experience and of its coincident illusory all-encompassing nature. Dzogchen may be described as simple perceptivity, and beyond intellectual comprehension, but surely never as naiveté.

The language of Vajrayana may be engaged as expression of the poetry of Dzogchen singing the songs of realization of the nature of mind. But Vajrayana technique provides multiple means of recognition of mind's nature and special techniques of removing karmic obstacles untouched and left behind by the light of initiatory experience. The technical creative and fulfilment stages of understanding,

*for example, allow all our common or garden experience
to be immediately incorporated into the totality-mandala
of the here and now. The infinite variety of totality-
mandalas represent composite mental states in terms of
the visual forms of the wrathful and peaceful deities.*

*Thus, in this Dzogchen context, visualization of the 100
wrathful and peaceful buddha-deities and recitation of
their mantric, sonic, form may be likened to the
homeopathic pills that are administered to the sick and
maladjusted – 'like cures like' (similar similibus curantor)
or perhaps 'like illuminates like' and thus renders all
things evanescent. Insofar as the likeness or symbolic
value of one of the 100 wrathful and peaceful deities
accords with a chronic dualizing state of mind, a
substantial nub of karmic potential may be dissolved. Like
a precious pill (rilbu), or a homeopathic remedy, a
wrathful or peaceful image may be administered as an
amplifier or illuminator that dissolves an obstacle – or
excrescence – into the clear light of reality.*

*The following description of the elements of the basic
vajrayana Vairochana-mandala provides a symbological
transmission of tantric initiation-empowerments.*

I The Existential Elements of the Mandala

1. *Relating to Dharmakaya*
The unitary Kuntuzangpo, Samantabhadra, the All-Good,
symbolizes the unity of the three kayas. The following
abstract nounal phrases all point at that unspeakable
totality:

Unity, nonduality
the zero-dimension
nonabiding awareness of the now
the field of 'A'
the clear light of all

the field of reality
present awareness
spaciousness/awareness
unitary sublime form
unitary dimensions (*trikaya*)
buddha

2. Relating to sambhogakaya
Fivefold Present Awareness
The unitary all-inclusive five
immutability and the unchanging, unimpeded field
sameness, and sameness of the field
compassionate creativity and a hot and devotional field
consummate activity and self-released field

Attributes of Nonduality
the five families and symbols
the forty-twofold psychophysical attributes
the five-colored light
immutability and noncrystalization
a vastness of potential
breadth and depth of wisdom
source of gnostic compassion
immaculate and stainless
immanent sublime vision
source of selfless activity.

The pure nature of:
the five body-mind aggregates
the five great elements
the five objective sensory fields
the five afflictive emotions.

3. Relating to nirmanakaya

The five fields of sensory perception (the fivefold objects
of consciousness) and the sense organs and
consciousnesses as nondual.

Compassion manifest as the eight consciousnesses and the eight fields of consciousness.

Pure presence manifests in the five aspects of present awareness and its ground of clarity as defined below:

pure presence of mirror-like awareness and the ground of its clarity; and unimpeded gaze and simultaneity of gaze and clarity: Charm and Flower;

pure presence of awareness of sameness and the ground of its clarity; and clarification of actual stains: Rosary (Garland) and Incense;

pure presence of discriminating awareness and the ground of its clarity; and ideation and its clarification: Song and Light;

pure presence of all-accomplishing awareness and the ground of its clarity; and what is born and the time of birth: Dance and Taste.

Freedom from the four misconceptions of reality as blissful, permanent, substantial and true;

freedom from the conceptual extremes of eternalism, nihilism, egoic self, and substantial nature;

endowment of the four boundless qualities: loving kindness, sympathetic joy, compassion and equanimity;

the activity of the six bodhisattva-siddhamunis emanated into the six realms, demonstrating the purity of passion and the purity of activity in their respective realms.

II The Forty-Two Sambhogakaya Buddha-Deities in Five Family Mandala Groups

The denomination of the five families is based firstly on spatial aspect and secondly on color. The adibuddha represents spatial unity and unity of time (nonspatial and timeless reality of the here and now). The Buddha Family represents the adibuddha manifest as multiplicity in space/time. The color white that relates to this family is the origin of all rainbow color and specifically to the four root colors of the directional four families.

In Dzogchen, particularly in the togal context, the colors are primary, symbolized by the five buddhas. The psychophysical constituents represented by those buddhas (internal) are in union with the great elements as their yums (external). The internal elements of perception – consciousnesses and organs – are represented by the eight bodhisattvas while the objects of perception are their female bodhisattva counterparts, the offering goddesses.

NB The contents of square brackets provide Longchen Nyingtik numerical values indicating the number of symbolic forms in that family.

Adibuddha [2]

Samantabhadra, Kuntuzangpo, Kun tu bzang po, the All-good adibuddha: present awareness.

Samantabhadri, Kuntuzangmo, Kun tu bzang mo, The All-good female adibuddha: the spaciousness of reality.

The unitary Kuntuzangpo, male and female adi-buddha united, spaciousness/awareness.

Buddha Family [2]

Vairochana, Nampar Nangdze, *Nam par snang mdzad,* Manifesting Universal Multiplicity: awareness of unitary space, WHITE, form aggregate: poison, ignorance (fear).

[Dhatishvari, Yingi Wongchukma, *Dbying gi dbang phyug ma,* Space-Lady, space element.]

Vajra Family [6]

Akshobhya, Mikyopa, *Mi skyod p*a: The Unshakeable, Immovable: BLUE, mirror-like awareness, consciousness aggregate: poison, anger.

Buddhalochana, Sangye Chenma, *Sang rgyas spyan ma*,
　　　Clear-Eyed Buddha: earth element.
Kshitigarbha, Sayinyingpo, *Sa yi snying po*, Earth-
　　　　　　Essence: presence of mirror-like awareness [eye
　　　　　　consciousness].
Maitreya, Jampa, *Byams pa*, Loving Kindness: clarity of
　　　　　　mirror-like awareness [organ of eye].
Lasya, Gekmoma, *Sgeg mo ma*, Charm: unimpeded gaze
　　　　　　[objects of form].
Pushpa, Metokma, *Me tog ma*, Flower: simultaneity of
　　　　　　gaze and clarity [thought of the past].

Jewel Family [6]

Ratnasambhava, Rinchenjungne, *Rin chen byung gnas*,
　　　　　　Jewel Source: YELLOW, awareness of sameness,
　　　　　　feeling aggregate (*vedana*): poison – pride.
Mamaki: water element.
Samantabhadra, Kuntuzangpo, *Kun tu bzang po*, All-
　　　　　　good: (bodhisattva) presence of awareness of
　　　　　　sameness [nose organ].
Akashagarbha, Namkhai Nyingpo, *Nam mkha'i snying
　　　　　　po*, Space-Essence: clarity of awareness of
　　　　　　sameness [nose consciousness].
Mala, Tengwa, *Phreng ba*, Rosary/Garland: clarification
　　　　　　of stains [objects of smell].
Gandha, Dukpoma, *Dug spos ma,* Incense: clarification
　　　　　　of stains [present thought].

Lotus Family [6]

Amitabha, Wopakme, *'Od dpag med*, Boundless Light:
　　　　　　RED, discriminating awareness, concept
　　　　　　aggregate: poison – desire.
Pandaravasini, *Dgos dkar can,* White Gown: fire
　　　　　　element.
Avalokiteshvara, Chenrezik, *Spyan ras gzigs*, Tearful
　　　　　　Gaze: discriminating awareness [tongue
　　　　　　consciousness].

Manjushri, Jampel, *'Jam dpal*, Tender Glory: clarity of
discriminating awareness [tongue organ].
Gita, Luma, *Glu ma*: Song: ideation [objects of sound].
Aloka, Marme, *Mar me*, Lamp: clarification of ideation
[thought of the future].

Vajra-Cross Family [6]

Amoghasiddhi, *Don yod grub pa*, All-Accomplisher:
GREEN, all-accomplishing awareness, volition
aggregate (*samskara*), jealousy.
Samayatara, Damtsik Drolma *Dam tshig sgrol ma,*
Commitment-Savioress: air element.
Vajrapani, Chaknadorje, *Phyag na rdo rje*, Vajra-in-Hand:
presence of all-accomplishing awareness [ear
consciousness].
Sarvanivarana-viskambhin, Dripanamsel, *Sgrib pa rnam
sel*, Cloud Dissolver: clarity of all-accomplishing
awareness [ear organ].
Nritya, Garma, *Gar m*a: Dance: what is born [objects of
sound].
Gandha, Drichabma, *Dri chab ma*: Taste: the time of birth
[abstract thought].

Doorkeepers [8]

The doorkeepers represent what appears externally to
beings who have not yet achieved initiatory experience of
the nature of mind. Internally, the doorkeepers symbolize
aspects of mind's nature.

Four Male doorkeepers: The male doorkeepers represent
freedom from the misconception that the deluded
experiences of samsara are permanent (*rtag*), true (*bden*),
pleasant (*bde ba*) and concrete (*mtshan ma*). [See Thinley
Norbu 1993].

Amritakundali – tactile consciousness,
Hayagriva – tactile sensation,

Mahabhala – body as a sensory organ,
Yamantaka – body-consciousness

Four Female Doorkeepers: The female doorkeepers
represent freedom from the four conceptual extremes of
eternalism, nihilism, egoism and materialism, *or* they
represent possession of the four boundless qualities of
equanimity, loving kindness, sympathetic joy and
compassion. [See Thinley Norbu, 1993]

The four female herukas in yab-yum union with the four
male doorkeepers are distinguished by the instrument that
they hold, each indicating a form of gross samsaric
bondage: *ankusha* – hook, *pasha* – noose, *sphota* – chain,
and *gantha* – bell.

Siddhamunis [6]

Mahindra, Vemachitra, Sakyamuni, Singha, Jvalamukha,
and Dharmaraja *aka* Yamaraja [see Thinley Norbu 1993];
Bodhisattva adepts of the six realms (gods, demons,
human beings, animals, hungry ghosts, devils).

Two seeming anomalies in this mandala attribution should
be noted: First, Dhatishvari, the consort of Vairochana, is
absent, and thus the forty-two attributes of sambhogakaya
are reduced to forty-one. The name Dhatishvari is not
mentioned in the tantra.

Secondly, the white color of Vairochana is associated with
the aggregate of form and the blue body of Akshobhya is
associated with consciousness, whereas a logical
denomination would reverse these attributions. Likewise, a
logical designation would associate earth with form and
space with consciousness. This apparent inconsistency is
resolved by the recognition of form as light (or 'lightform')
and consciousness as a mere passive function. In later
more sophisticated mandalas, the places of Akshobhya
(frequently as Vajrasattva) and Vairochana would be
reversed.

III The Forty-two Sublime Forms in *Trikaya* Grouping

Trikaya implies the innate body of emptiness, the unitary body, which can be conceived and categorized according to either an epistemological or ontological approach. Here the ontological approach distinguishes three categories – mind, speech and body – as dharmakaya, sambhogakaya and nirmanakaya and then distinguishes three degrees, again denominated as dharmakaya, sambhogakaya and nirmanakaya. Regarding this classification of trikaya:

Firstly, *dharmakaya trikaya*

Changeless, unidentifiable presence is *dharmakaya* dimension of *dharmakaya*. Uninterrupted intuition of presence as the five sublime forms of wisdom is the *sambhogakaya* enjoyment-dimension of *dharmakaya*. The five sublime forms emanating as 'what is converted' is the magical *nirmanakaya* dimension of *dharmakaya*.

Dharmakaya trikaya is also called 'the triad of essence, nature and compassion' (*ngo bo rang bzhin thugs rje gsum*); 'the three existential dimensions inherent' (*gzhi la gnas pa'i sku gsum*); 'the presence of fruition in the ground' (*'bras bu gzhi la grub pa*); 'the great inversion of trikaya' (*sku gsum ja log chen po*); and also 'fruition within fruition' (*'bras bu 'bras bu'i ngang la gnas pa*).

Secondly, *sambhogakaya trikaya:*
The all-inclusive *dharmakaya* dimension of *sambhogakaya* is Mahavairochana, the Universal Illuminator. The *sambhogakaya* enjoyment dimension of *sambhogakaya* is composed of the members of the four families. The magical *nirmanakaya* dimension of *sambhogakaya* is composed of the male and female bodhisattvas.

Their different epithets are: 'the moment of clearly manifest fruition' (*'bras bu mngon par gsal ba'i dus*) and

'differentiated *trikaya*' (*sku gsum rnam par gzhag pa*).
Such are the three dimensions of *sambhogakaya*.

Sambhogakaya–Dharmakaya
Mahavairochana ('The Sixth')

Sambhogakaya–Sambhogakaya
Vairochana, Nampar Nangdze, *Nam par snang mdzad,*
    Multiplicitous Manifestation
Akshobhya, Mikyopa, *Mi skyod pa,* The Unshakeable,
    Indestructible
Amitabha, Wopakme, *'Od dpag med,* Boundless Light

Ratnasambhava, Rinchenjungne, *Rin chen byung gnas,*
    Fountain of Jewels
Amoghasiddhi, Donyodrupa, *Don yod grub pa,* All-
    Accomplisher.
Dhatishvari, Yingi Wongchukma, *Dbying gi dbang phyug
    ma,* Space-Lady, space element.
Buddhalochana, Sangye Chenma, *Sang rgyas spyan ma,*
    Clear-Eyed Buddha.
Pandaravasini, Gokarmo, *Dgos dkar mo,* White Gown.
Mamaki.
Samayatara, Damtsik Drolma, *Dam tshig sgrol ma,*
    Commitment-Savioress.

Sambhogakaya–Nirmanakaya
Samantabhadra, Kuntuzangpo, *Kun tu bzang po* (All-
    Good).
Akashagarbha, Namkhai Nyingpo, *Nam mkha'i
    snying po,* Sky-Essence.
Kshitigarbha, Sayinyingpo, *Sa'i snying po,* Earth-
    Essence.
Maitreya, Jampa, Byams pa, Loving Kindness.
Avalokiteshvara, Chenrezik, *Spyan ras gzigs,* Tearful Eyes.
Manjushri, Jampel, 'Jam dpal, Tender Glory.
Vajrapani, Chaknadorje, *Phyag na rdo rje,*
    Vajra-in-Hand.
Sarvanivarana-viskambhin, Dripanamsel, *Sgrib pa rnam
    sel,* Cloud Dissolver.

Gita (Song), Aloka (Light), Lasya (Charm), Pushpa (Flower), Mala (Garland), Dhupa (Incense), Nritya (Dance), Gandha (Taste).

Thirdly, *nirmanakaya trikaya:*

The four families represent the *dharmakaya* dimension of *nirmanakaya*. Male and female bodhisattvas represent the *sambhogakaya* dimension of enjoyment. The spreading light of nondual compassion is the dimension of magical *nirmanakaya* emanation [see *Everything is Light* ch. 31].

IV The Fifty-four Wrathful Deities

The term 'wrathful', although a literal rendering of the Tibetan trowa (khro ba or Sanskrit krodha), in Dzogchen implies simple activity, or hyperactivity, rather than aspects of anger or desire, which are its rendering in any dualistic approach. Dzogchen mollifies the emotional aspect leaving only the active form that is depicted so dramatically in Tibetan zhitro art.

Of the fifty-four, only the five herukas and their consorts are graphically depicted with the third eye, indicating buddha-nature, but in the Dzogchen mandala, since there is no distinction in degrees of manifestation, all forms are equally of ultimate nondual nature.

All fifty-four are representations of compassionate buddha manifesting spontaneously to illuminate an all-encompassing moment of the here and now. Whereas the herukas, the seemingly demonic forms, represent totality-moments as described in the various root-tantras, the more recognizably human forms, part animal or demonic, may depict negative emotional elements, or scrambled energy, tangled karmic imprints, body-mind syndromes that have been 'released' or recognized as perfect in their nature and necessary as an aspect of the whole. Particularly, the Wongchukma represent the knots in the mind, karmic tendencies, that have been dissolved, or illuminated.

*Note that apart from the five heruka consorts of the five krodhas and the four consorts of the four female gatekeepers, nine in all, forty-five of the wrathful deities are female. In the yabyum vortex the female gender indicates the objective aspect of every perceptual situation. In the dynamic yabyum moment, 'subjective' refers to pure awareness (rigpa) and 'objective' refers to the unitary interior/exterior form (*ying*).*

The Five Wrathful Herukas and Consorts [10]

Buddha-heruka with his consort Buddha-krodhishvari;
Vajra-heruka with his consort Vajra-krodhishvari;
Ratna-heruka with his consort Ratna-krodhishvari;
Padma-heruka with his consort Padma-krodhishvari;
Karma-heruka with his consort Karma-krodhishvari.

The Eight Gaurima, Wrathful Female Deities [8]

These are the names of eight Newar devis, which are very angry protectresses:

Gauri;
Pukasi (Protectress of the Boudha Stupa);
Chaurimatrika;
Ghasmari;
Pramoha;
Chandali;
Vetali (ghoul or ghost);
Shmashani (cremation ground goblin).

The Eight Tramen (*Piśacī*: flesh-eating and shape-changing demonesses with animal heads). [8]

Singhamukha   (Lion-head)
Vyaghrimukha (Tigress-head)
Sringalamukha (Horn-head)
Shvanamukha; (Dog-head)

Gridhamukha   (Vulture-head)
Kangkamukha (Unicorn-head?)
Kakamukha   (Crow-head)
Ulumukha   (Owl-head)

The Four Gatekeeper-Couples [8] (Gomazhi, *Sgo ma bzhi*).
This reckoning includes the four principal Herukas of the
four primary Newar tantras in union with four *yum*
protectresses.

Achala, the exclusively protective form of
Chandamaharosana, in union with Ankusha, Iron-Hook-
Lady (Chakyuma, *Lcags kyu ma*), otherwise Horse-
headed-Bitch (Tadongma, *Rta gdong ma*) guardian of the
eastern gate.

Vajrabhairava or Yamantaka (Shinjeshe, *Gshin rje shed*)
in union with Pasha, Noose-Lady (Zhakpama, *Zhags pa
ma*), otherwise Sow-headed-Bitch (Phakdongma, *Phag
gdong ma*, guardian of the southern gate.

Hayagriva (Tamdrin, *Rta mgrin*) in union with Shrinkhala,
Iron Chain-Lady (Chakdrokma, *Lcags sgrog
ma*), otherwise Lion-headed-Bitch (Sengdongma, *Seng
gdong ma*), guardian of the western gate.

Amritakundali (Dutsimen, *Bdud rtsi sman*) in union
with Ghanta, Bell-Lady, (Drilbuma, *Dril bu ma*),
otherwise Jackal-faced-Bitch (Jangdongma, *Spyang gdong
ma*), guardian of the northern gate.

The Twenty-four Wongchukma (Skt. Ishvarī; *Dbang
phyug ma)* [24]

*The twenty-four Wongchukma are devi-like entities, demi-
goddesses and their categoric name, Ishwari, implies a
Hindu origin. In many of the twenty-four, a Sanskritic
name invokes a partial aspect of an original Hindu god or
goddess rather than a complete traditional divine entity.
In the remainder, identity as the original numinous Hindu
entity implied by the name is belied by the form in its*

mandala depiction. Thus the twenty-four names are suggestive of a mixed Hindu-Buddhist culture such as the Newar Kathmandu Valley or the Assamese Brahmaputra Valley. However, despite their Sanskritic names, their representation in Tibetan tankas and murals is Tibetan in origin. Unless we have intimate association with Himalayan culture and its numinous cultural forms it would be most useful to identify these twenty-four Ishwari as enlightened manifestations of our own western cultural archetypes. Whatever the forms, these archetypes should be identified, as yogini-protectors that are divided into four groups of six relating to the four buddha-activities of pacifying, enriching, enslaving and destroying, respectively:

Rakshasi	White ogress
Brahmi	Consort of Brahma, the Creator
Mahadevi	Uma, consort of the Great God Shiva
Lobha	'Greed'
Kumari	The Virgin, consort of Kumar
Indrani	Consort of Indra, king of the gods
Vajra	'Adamantine'
Shanti	'Peace'
Amrita	'Ambrosia'
Chandra	Goddess of the Moon
Danda	'Staff'
Rakshasi	Ochre ogress
Bhakshini	'Ghost-demon'
Rati	Goddess of the Night
Mahabala	'Great Strength'
Rakshasi	Pink ogress
Kama	'Sexual Desire'
Vasuraksha	The Krishna Demon

Vayudevi	Wind Goddess
Nari	Female
Varahi	Sow Goddess
Nanda	'The Bull'
Mahahastini	'Great Cow-Elephant'
Varunadevi	Water Goddess.

The Prayer of the Three Yogas:
The Braided Vajra-Knot

As the mindstream of lama and yidam deities,
the merit of diligence accomplished here and now,
and the merit accumulated in past, present and future –
all our merit – is dedicated to supreme enlightenment.

While we attain the heart of enlightenment,
born in a good family, with clear mind and humility,
with great compassion devoted to the guru,
we remain secure in the glorious Vajrayana.

Matured through initiatory experience, samaya bound,
completing visualisation and recitation on the paths of
    development and fulfilment,
without difficulty reaching the level of rigdzin,
we easily attain realization and magical powers.

All appearances perfected within the circle of the net of
    ceaselessly transforming emanation,
all sound the inexpressible vibration of mantra,
all mind-movement uncompounded intrinsic awareness –
we fully experience ever-present supreme bliss.

Recognizing faults and failings and defiling thoughts
    as pure as they stand,
fulfilled through realisation of outside, inside and secret
    undifferentiated,

whatever arises self-liberated in the vast expanse of
     Kuntuzangpo,
samsara and nirvana identical, the depths of hell are
     emptied.

Pure being and visionary fields perfected in the cosmic
     seed,
concrete judgment purified in the great samaya,
knots of hope and fear untied in all-encompassing
     spaciousness,
the dharmakaya is revealed in the Great Perfection.

The blessings of the three lineages suffusing our heart,
the secret path of transforming illusion perfected in our
     mind,
through spontaneous accomplishment of the four
     buddha-karmas,
all innumerable, boundless, beings are liberated.

Guided by the circle of wrathful and peaceful emanation,
protected like children by the dakinis,
all obstacles removed by the guardian-protectors,
may all our prayers be fulfilled,
may the buddha-teaching spread and extend,
may doctrine-holders' ambition be accomplished,
may the hardships of all beings be relieved,
and their minds endowed with sublime virtue.

May this great secret, sealed as buddha,
this peerless, supreme teaching,
spread and extend throughout the world,
like the sun shining high in the sky.

The Lady Yeshe Tsogyel
and the Seven Thieves

*These excerpts from Yeshe Tsogyel's life-story provide
extraordinary evidence of her transcendent awareness and
compassion. In her encounter with the seven thieves, we
may understand Tsogyel as the personification of primal
awareness and the seven thieves as clear light forms.*

Yeshe Tsogyel tells her story:

I received my Guru's prophetic injunction, and with a
golden begging bowl and a pound of gold dust, I set out
alone for the Kathmandu Valley. In the district of Erong I
encountered seven thieves. They sought to steal my gold,
and followed me like dogs stalking a deer. I invoked my
Guru and visualized the thieves as my Yidam, and
conceiving the perfect plan of rendering my possessions as
a mandala offering, inspired I sang to them:

"O Seven Yidam of Erong,
it is so fortunate to meet you today.
for thereby I attain buddha
and fulfil the wishes of all sentient beings.
Now let karmic misadventure be swiftly transformed
to discover, fortuitously, the lama's compassion!
How truly marvelous that will be!
Happy thoughts arising within
may people find freedom through giving!"

I arranged my gold in a mandala pile and placed my hands together in reverence. The seven thieves could not understand a word but touched by the melody of my song, they stood staring at me like statues, transported to the first level of samadhi. Then, in the Newar language, one of them asked me, "What is your country, Venerable Lady? Who is your father? Who is your mother? Who is your Lama? What are you doing here? Please sing us another song!"

As they made this request, their body-hair that had bristled in aggression lay down, a wreath of happy smiles signified their satisfaction, their malicious twisted faces became serene, and their pleasure showed in garlands of teeth. Gathering in front of me they sat down and leaning upon my triple-jointed bamboo cane I replied in their Newar tongue:

"You seven thieves, my karmic desserts,
know aggression and malice as mirror-like awareness –
radiant clarity has no other source
than a hostile mind filled with enmity and anger.

"Look into your anger
for there is the strength of Vajrasattva,
and detached from appearances
you are purified in emptiness.

"This maiden's fatherland is Overflowing Joy,
serene fields of emptiness and visionary pleasure;
I am no stickler for names and forms
so if this lady's fair land appeals to you,
let us go there together.

"You seven thieves, my karmic desserts,
know that pride and complacency are awareness of
        sameness –
primal purity in composure can nowhere be found
except in an ambitious, overweening mind.

"Look into natural purity,
the fountain of jewels that is Ratnasambhava,
and in the detachment of emptiness,
light-form is pure.

"This maiden's father, the source of every gratification,
    is nothing but the wish-fulfilling gem itself;
I am no glutton for the illusory chattels of wealth
so if you fancy these riches take them all from me.

"You seven thieves, my karmic desserts,
know that desire and greed are discriminating
        awareness—
you will find fine sensory distinction in no other place
than in desire for beauty, in beauty itself.

"Look into the intrinsic freshness of desire,
the boundless light of Amitabha,
and detached from the radiance
our pleasure is pure.

"This maiden's mother is that Boundless Light
and in her is endless pure pleasure;
I am no votary of the sparkle of feeling
so if this sweet lady appeals to you,
take her from me.

"You seven thieves, my karmic desserts,
Know that alienation and envy are all-accomplishing
        awareness –
efficiency and success have no other source
than bigotry, quick to judge, holding a grudge.

"Look behind jealous thoughts,
at immediate success, Amoghasiddhi,
and detached from crass envy and subtle resentment,
the nature of whatever occurs is pure.

"This maiden's lama is Spontaneous Accomplishment,
the lama whose actions are invariably consummate;
and since I am no slave to my work
if you want this diligent lama
take him from me.

"You seven thieves, my karmic deserts,
know that ignorance and stupidity are awareness of
        space –
there is no better way to hold fast to the path
than through ignorance and stupidity.

"Look into ignorance
and there is the visionary panorama of Vairochana,
and detached from hypnotic ignorance,
whatever arises is pure.

"This maiden's beloved is Visionary Panorama,
my ultimate consort, the Illuminator;
and transcending the duality of vision and viewer,
if you desire my service I will show you the way."

The thieves, repulsed from the wheel of rebirth, were
filled with undivided faith. They begged me for
instruction and precepts, and thereby gained release from
samsara. Then they entreated me insistently to come with
them to their own country, but I refused and continued on
my way

Yeshe Tsogyel's Song of the Four Joys

This song of the four joys is also the song of the four initiations. It is a moot point whether purely ritual initiation-empowerment can provide experiential knowledge of the nature of mind. Perhaps the most sought-after rituals that the lamas offer are merely conceptual allegories of four stages of initiation providing foreknowledge that can smooth the way for the existential reality. Certainly in this lyrical replay of the rape inflicted upon her, Tsogyel affirms that sexual experience can contain the elements of Dzogchen initiatory experience and then by extension the affirmation that any experience – if possessing sufficient illumination (or intensity?) – can provide certainty that the nature of mind is available within it, that every sensory experience is an expression of buddha.

We should not ignore the possibility, however, that these verses are couched in 'twilight language' (sandhyabhasa), where sexual innuendo and technical tantric language hide an exposition of simple sensory experience, which can be found in the Buddhist abhidharma shastras in a more forthright language.

What is lacking in the technical abhidharma *of both Hinayana and Mahayana and what is larded upon this tantric exposition is the mystic sense that is best described as 'great compassion'. What other than truly transcendental compassion could turn rape into a parable of generosity and loving kindness?*

Then I, Yeshe Tsogyel, went to live in Shampo Gang, and it was there that seven bandits robbed me of my possessions and raped me.

Afterwards I sang them this song of introduction to the four joys:

NAMO GURU PADMA SIDDHI HRĪ!

Good friends,
by chance you have met a sublime consort, your goddess,
and by virtue of your resources of accumulated merit,
fortuitously, you have received the four initiations.
Now focus on the issue of the four levels of joy!

Immediately you set eyes on my body-mandala
your minds were possessed by lust
and that confidence won you the vase initiation.
Apprehend the very essence of lust,
identify it as your creative vision of the deity,
and that is nothing but the *yidam* deity itself:
meditate upon lustful mind as divine being.

Uniting with the space in your consort's secret mandala,
pure pleasure exciting your nerve centers,
your aggression was assuaged, loving kindness arising,
and its power won you the mystic initiation.
Apprehend the very essence of joy,
mix it with your vital energy and maintain it,
and if that is not mahamudra, nothing is:
experience pleasure as mahamudra,

Joined to your consort's sphere of pure pleasure,
inspired to involuntary exertion,
your mind merges with my mind,
and that blessing wins you the wisdom initiation.
Undistracted, guard the very essence of pleasure,
identify pure pleasure with emptiness,
and that is what is known as immaculate empty pleasure:
experience pure pleasure as supreme joy.

United at your consort's blissful nerve,
our two nectars fuse into one elixir.
The phenomena of self and others extinguished,
awareness won you the initiation of creative expression.
Guard the natural purity in the world of appearances,
identify your love and attachment with emptiness,
and that is nothing other than Dzogchen itself:
experience innate joy as no-joy.

This extraordinary exalted secret instruction,
consciously practiced brings a fall;
discovered adventitiously it gives miraculous release:
you have attained the four initiations at once,
and your success is matured by the four stages of joy.

Licchabi Vimalakirti Nirdesha Sutra:
A Dzogchen Rendition

Here in this the most Zen-like of the mahayana sutras, most treasured by the Far-Eastern Buddhist sangha, the bodhisattva of wisdom, Manjushri, requires the mahayana sangha of Vimalakirti to express their understanding of nonduality. Imbued with Dzogchen realization, the sangha expresses themselves admirably in the metaphysical abhidharmic language of their era, only to be outclassed by Vimalakirti himself who expresses himself in the language of silence similar to that attributed to Sakyamuni's disciple Kasyapa who sits in silence holding a flower in order to express the nature of mind, and by so doing incidentally he establishes the Chan/Zen lineage.

In this rendition I have edited the sutra to serve the vision of Dzogchen. The five hundred bodhisattvas of Vimalakirti's sangha are no longer outside seeking a method to attain entry, they are inside seeking to divest themselves of their realization of the experience of being there. Please note that that state of looking out from within is not yet the Dzogchen view in which inside and outside are united in a nondual reality. That unified natural condition is demonstrated only by Vimalakirti's silence, like Kasyapa's presentation of the flower, which is a manner of expressing the nonconceptual, supra-verbal, state of Dzogchen realization.

Then the Licchabi Manjushri made this request to the congregation of bodhisattvas: "Good sirs, please explain

how all beings abide within the dharma-door of
nonduality!"

And the venerable congregation replied one after the
other in this manner:

"Noble sir, production and destruction are two, but what
is not produced and does not occur cannot be destroyed.
Thus the natural tolerance of the birthlessness of things
places all beings within the dharma-door of nonduality."

"'I' and 'mine' are two. But there is no presumption of a
self, so there is no possessiveness. Thus, absence of
presumption places all beings within the dharma-door of
nonduality."

"'Defilement' and 'purification' are two. But when there
is thorough knowledge of defilement, there is no conceit
about purification. The path leading to the complete
conquest of all conceit is the no-path within the dharma-
door of nonduality."

"'Distraction' and 'attention''are two. But when there is
no distraction, there is no attention, no mentation, and no
mental intensity. Thus, in absence of mental intensity lies
nonduality."

"'Bodhisattva spirit' and 'disciple spirit' are two. But
when both are seen to resemble an illusory spirit, there is
no bodhisattva spirit, nor any disciple spirit. Thus,
'sameness of natures of spirits' describes nonduality."

"'Grasping' and 'nongrasping' are two. But what is not
grasped is not perceived, and what is not perceived is
neither presumed nor repudiated. Thus, in the inaction
and non-involvement of all things lies nonduality."

"'Uniqueness' and 'characterlessness' are two. But not to
presume or construct something is neither to establish its
uniqueness nor to establish its characterlessness. To
recognize the equality of these two is nonduality."

"'Good' and 'evil' are two. But seeking neither good nor evil, the understanding of the nonduality of the significant and the meaningless is the reality of nonduality."

"'Sinfulness' and 'sinlessness' are two. But by virtue of the diamond-like wisdom that suffuses the very essence, not to be bound or liberated is the nature of nonduality. "To say, 'this is impure' and 'that is immaculate' makes for duality. One who knows equanimity, forms no conception of impurity or immaculateness, yet is not utterly without conception, has equanimity without any attainment of equanimity – he is void of conceptual knots. Thus, he abides in nonduality."

"To say, 'this is happiness' and 'that is misery' is dualism. One who is free of all calculations, through the extreme purity of gnosis – his mind is aloof, like empty space; and thus he abides in nonduality."

"To say, 'this is mundane' and 'that is transcendental' is dualism. But this world has the nature of voidness, so there is neither transcendence nor involvement, neither progress nor standstill. Thus, neither to transcend nor to be involved, neither to go nor to stop – this is to abide in nonduality."

"'Life' and 'liberation' are dualistic. Having seen the nature of life, one neither belongs to it nor is one utterly liberated from it. Such understanding emanates from nonduality."

"'Destructible' and 'indestructible' are dualistic. But what is destroyed is ultimately destroyed. What is ultimately destroyed does not become destroyed; hence, it is called 'indestructible'. What is indestructible is instantaneous, and what is instantaneous is indestructible. The experience of such is called 'understanding the principle of nonduality'."

"'Self' and 'selflessness' are dualistic. But since the existence of self cannot be perceived, what is there to be made 'selfless'? Thus, in nondual vision of their nature lies nonduality."

"'Knowledge' and 'ignorance' are dualistic. But the natures of ignorance and knowledge are the same, for ignorance is undefined, incalculable, and beyond the sphere of thought. In the realization of this lies nonduality."

"Matter itself is void. Voidness does not result from the destruction of matter, but the nature of matter is itself voidness. Therefore, to speak of voidness on the one hand, and of matter, or of sensation, or of intellect, or of motivation, or of consciousness on the other, is entirely dualistic. Consciousness itself is voidness. Voidness does not result from the destruction of consciousness, but the nature of consciousness is itself voidness. Such understanding of the five compulsive aggregates and the knowledge of them as such by means of gnosis arises out of nonduality."

"To say that the four main elements are one thing and the etheric space-element another is dualistic. The four main elements are themselves the nature of space. The past itself is also the nature of space. The future itself is also the nature of space. Likewise, the present itself is also the nature of space. The gnosis that penetrates the elements in such a way arises in nonduality."

"'Eye' and 'form' are dualistic. To understand the eye correctly, and not to have attachment, aversion, or confusion with regard to form – that is called 'peace'. Similarly, 'ear' and 'sound', 'nose' and 'smell', 'tongue' and 'taste', 'body' and 'touch', and 'mind' and 'phenomena' – all are dualistic. But to know the mind, and to be neither attached, averse, nor confused with regard to phenomena – that is called 'peace'. To live in such peace is to rest in nonduality."

"The dedication of generosity for the sake of attaining omniscience is dualistic. The nature of generosity is itself omniscience, and the nature of omniscience itself is total dedication. Likewise, it is dualistic to dedicate morality, tolerance, effort, meditation, and wisdom for the sake of omniscience. Omniscience is the nature of wisdom, and total dedication is the nature of omniscience. Thus, understanding this principle of uniqueness is to understand nonduality."

"It is dualistic to say that voidness is one thing, signlessness another, and wishlessness still another. What is void has no sign. What has no sign has no wish. Where there is no wish there is no process of thought, mind, or consciousness. To see the doors of all liberations in the door of one liberation is to know nonduality."

"It is dualistic to say 'Buddha,' 'Dharma,' and 'Saṅgha.' The Dharma is itself the nature of the Buddha, the Saṅgha is itself the nature of the Dharma, and all of them are uncompounded. The uncompounded is infinite space, and the processes of all things are equivalent to infinite space. Knowledge of this is to know nonduality."

"It is dualistic to refer to 'aggregates' and to the 'cessation of aggregates'. Aggregates themselves are cessation. Why? The egoistic views of aggregates, being unproduced themselves, do not exist ultimately. Hence such views do not really conceptualize 'these are aggregates' or 'these aggregates cease'. Ultimately, they have no such discriminative constructions and no such conceptualizations. Therefore, such views have themselves the nature of cessation. Nonoccurrence and nondestruction are the nature of nonduality."

"Physical, verbal, and mental vows do not exist dualistically. Why? These things have the nature of inactivity. The nature of inactivity of the body is the same as the nature of inactivity of speech, whose nature of inactivity is the same as the nature of inactivity of the mind.

"It is necessary to know and to understand this fact of the ultimate inactivity of all things, for this knowledge is knowledge of nonduality."

"It is dualistic to consider actions meritorious, sinful, or unmoving. The non-undertaking of meritorious, sinful, and unmoving actions is not dualistic. The intrinsic nature of all such actions is voidness, wherein ultimately there is neither merit, nor sin, nor non-movement, nor action itself. The nonaccomplishment of such actions is the reality of nonduality."

"Dualism is produced from obsession with self, whereas true understanding of self does not result in dualism. Who thus abides in nonduality is without ideation, and that absence of ideation is the nature of nonduality."

"Duality is constituted by perceptual manifestation. Nonduality is objectlessness. Therefore, nongrasping and nonrejection are the signs of nonduality."

"'Darkness' and 'light' are dualistic, but the absence of both darkness and light is nonduality. Why? At the time of absorption in cessation, there is neither darkness nor light, and likewise with the natures of all things. This equanimity is the nature of nonduality."

"It is dualistic to detest the world and to rejoice in liberation, and neither detesting the world nor rejoicing in liberation is nonduality. Why? Liberation can be found where there is bondage, but where there is ultimately no bondage where is the need for liberation?

The mendicant who is neither bound nor liberated does not experience any like or any dislike and thus rests in nonduality."

"It is dualistic to speak of 'good paths' and 'bad paths'. One who is on 'the path' is not concerned with good or bad paths. Living in such unconcern, he entertains no concepts of 'path' or 'nonpath'. Understanding the nature of concepts, his mind does not engage in duality. Such is the nature of nonduality."

"It is dualistic to speak of 'true' and 'false'. When one sees truly, one does not ever see any truth, so how could one see falsehood? Why? One does not see with the physical eye, one sees with the eye of wisdom. And with the wisdom-eye one sees only insofar as there is neither sight nor nonsight. There, where there is neither sight nor nonsight, is the nature of nonduality."

When the bodhisattvas had given their explanations, they all addressed the crown prince Manjushri, "Manjushri, what is the bodhisattva's experience of nonduality?"

And Manjushri replied, "Good sirs, you have all spoken well. Nevertheless, all your explanations are themselves dualistic. To know no one teaching, to express nothing, to say nothing, to explain nothing, to announce nothing, to indicate nothing, and to designate nothing – that is to rest in nonduality."

Then the crown prince Manjushri said to the Licchabi Vimalakirti, "We have all given our own teachings, noble sir. Now, may you, Vimalakirti, elucidate the teaching on the nature of the principle of nonduality!"

Thereupon, the Licchabi Vimalakirti kept his silence, saying nothing at all.

The crown prince Manjushri applauded the Licchabi Vimalakirti: "Excellent! Excellent, noble sir! This indeed is revelation of the nonduality of the bodhisattvas. Here, we have no use of syllables, sounds, and ideas."

When these teachings had been declared, five thousand bodhisattvas found themselves within the door of the dharma of nonduality and attained tolerance of the birthlessness of all things.

The Bodhisattva Vow

We vow to do whatsoever is necessary for the benefit of
whomsoever is in need.

[*To be repeated ritually three times*]

Arousal of Bodhichitta

Essence of the Mahayana

Precious Human Body
We assume human psychology, placing tantric methods for
    rebirth in abeyance.
We acknowledge our present body-mind as the precious
    human body, the vehicle for transcendence.
We bask in the good fortune of a good rebirth and good
    karma.

Eight Freedoms
We rejoice in:
freedom from rebirth in hell, rebirth as a preta, rebirth as an
    animal, rebirth as a god, rebirth as a titan
rebirth with intelligence and sensitivity
rebirth with learning and spiritual guidance
the notion of liberation and attainment of buddha.

Beneficial Conditions
With the such freedom, with a human birth, we recognize
    also:
a dharmic environment

a complete and functional body/mind
the absence of the inexpiable sins of killing father, mother,
    arhat, wounding a tathagata, or causing a schism
devotion to dharma
living in a buddha's world
availability of revealed dharma teaching
possibility of refuge in the triple gem
accessibility of spiritual friends and teachers
a good mind, good intention, good motivation
compassion
ready confession of faults and mistakes, shame and guilt
sensitivity and self-awareness
good karmic connections
the suffering inherent in birth, sickness, old age and death
controllable lust.

The Four Stations of Brahma and The Four Boundless Qualities
caturbrahmavihara: tshangs pa bzhi
and *caturapramana: tshad med bzhi*:

Purpose and Product

Recitation of the Chaturbrahmavihar and Contemplation
of the Four Boundless Qualities neutralizes the eight
mundane obsessions – pleasure and pain, fame and
ignominy, praise and blame, profit and loss.

Contemplation of the four boundless qualities is 'the sole
cause of attaining basic meditation stages'.

Practice results in 'streamwinner' status which is the
hinayana equivalent of attainment of initiatory experience,
or in tantra (*Hevajratantra*), attainment of the first stage
of 'pleasure'.

Boundless Equanimity
upeksha: btang snyoms

We begin with *upeksha*, the fourth in the formal verse:

Equanimity is an antidote to attachment and aversion, to
infatuation/attachment to friends and an antidote to
aversion/hatred to enemies. Equanimity for all is thus the
ground of the following three boundless qualities.

Each man's death diminishes me, For I
am involved in mankind. Therefore,
send not to know
For whom the bell tolls,
It tolls for thee.
(John Donne via Ernest Hemmingway)

Consider the friends who were once our enemies:
the mother who gave me birth,
the father who protected me,
the lover who gave me pleasure,
the doctor who saved my life,
the friend who loaned me money when I was broke.

Consider the enemies who were once our friends:
the guy who robbed my house,
the junkie who mugged me,
the motorist who knocked down my child,
the slanderer who spread lies about me,
the guy who stole my partner.

Equanimity as a sense of the compassionate equality of all
    sentient beings.

Metaphor: like a rishi (donor) giving alms to all equally;
    like giving offerings to all-comers (beggars around the
    Boudha stupa).

'May all beings attain immeasurable equanimity free of
attachment and aversion, both near and far'

Loving Kindness, Benevolence
maitri: byams pa

Conjure the love of a parent for his/her children
and of the love of children for parents.

Metaphor: consider the love of parents for intractable
          children,
recall disobedient, ungrateful, ignorant children,
the constant accepting, enduring, love of Jesus Christ,
parental self-sacrifice,
women and children first (saved in the Titanic disaster).

Like the love of a mother bird for her young: making a
nest, feeding them, protecting them with her wings, until
they can fly away, all without attachment.

May we want happiness for others as we want it for
ourselves.

Love of body, speech and mind:
Whenever I set eyes on another person
May my regard be always full of love.

Through all my lives, may I never harm a single hair of
the head of another being and may I always be of help to
each of them.

'May all beings be happy attaining the cause of
happiness'.

Compassion
karuna, snying rje

Invoke pathetic images inducing compassion:
the guilty criminal bound for execution,
Jews to the gas chamber,
sufferers with terminal diseases: AIDS and cancer,
animals at the butchers,
hungry ghosts (*pretas*): the addict without his fix.

Mother without arms watching her son being swept away
by a river, and then running along the river bank after him.

Empathy for all those tied to the wheel of samsara: 'There
but for the grace of god go I'.

John Bradford (1510-55) on watching a criminal en route to the gallows: "But for the grace of god there goes John Bradford."

'May all beings be free from suffering and the cause of suffering'.

<u>Sympathetic Joy</u>
mudita: dga' ba

As the antidote to jealousy:
Think of someone with every conceivable luxury and advantage,
someone with every talent and intelligence,
someone with beauty and charm,
someone with every comfort and servants,
those with happiness and long life:

wish for their increase in wealth and happiness,
wish that everyone else attains that same enviable state,
wish that one's partner enjoy extra-relational communication.

Think of a friend and wish every good upon that person,
every success, happiness, wealth and long life,
think of someone for whom you have indifferent feelings
and wish upon him/her the same enviable conditions,
think of someone you dislike and wish the same.

Imagine a mother camel finding her young lost in the desert.

'May all beings never be separate from the cause of happiness beyond suffering'.

The Siddha Bhandepa

Non-attachment is the highest form of loving kindness;
Realization of the nature of existence is compassion;
Inexhaustible pleasure is sympathetic joy;
And the ubiquitous one taste is perfect equanimity.

Bhandepa was a god living in the sky among the clouds of Shravasti. One day to his vast surprise he saw an apparition dressed in a monk's robes, carrying a begging bowl in one hand and a staff in the other, floating past him, radiating a divine aura.

"What is this god-like phenomenon floating through the sky," he asked Vishvakarman, Lord of the Gods.

"It is a saintly arhat, one who has cleansed himself of all passion," replied Vishvakarman.

Bhandepa yearned to emulate such accomplishment, and he descended to our world of the Rose Apple Tree to find a teacher. He found Krishnacharya and begged him for instruction. The master initiated him into the Guhyasamaja-mandala and taught him the yogin's protection – the four boundless states of mind: compassion as the ultimate vision, sympathetic joy as meditation, loving kindness as perfect action, and equanimity as the goal of his practice. Through his meditation Bhandepa cleansed his mind of all delusion, and he gained mahamudra-siddhi. He became famous as the yogin Bhandepa.

When Vishvakarman saw Bhandepa return to the sky above Shravasti he demanded to know what he had attained. Bhandepa replied:

I have attained the view that is without substance,
meditation that is unremitting,
action that is like a parent's affection,
and the goal that is like the sky.

When these four are recognized as one,
where can desire lodge?
How wonderful is the Guru!
The wise man will always serve him.

For four hundred years Bhandepa served the people of the six great towns of Aryavarta: Shravasti, Rajagrha, Vaisali, Varanasi, Pataliputra and Kanyakubja. Then with four hundred disciples he bodily attained the Dakini's Paradise.

Commentary

The irrelevance of sectarian divisions in Tantra is shown in this legend, where the arch-tantrika Krishnacharya gives Bhandepa, an admirer of the Hinayana, a tantric initiation and mahayana precepts that nevertheless give him mahamudra-siddhi. From the mahayana standpoint, technically, an arhat is he who observes impeccable manners, restraining himself from any reaction when reviled, angered, beaten or irritated, possessing few desires, practicing scrupulously modest behavior, eating moderately, and keeping from sleep in the first and last parts of the night. He has meditated upon all phenomena as essentially free of both positive and negative attributes, and as impermanent, sign-less, wish-less, and empty, then analyzing them into the five psycho-physical constituents, the five elements and the five sense-fields; and he has pondered the four noble truths in every way possible. To neutralize the three poisons he has contemplated their antidotes, such as the ugly and repulsive as the antidote to desire. He practices the thirty-seven topics conducive to enlightenment, and contemplates the twelve-fold chain of

interdependent origination. He has achieved deliverance
from the three realms of samsara, his nirvana is extinction
and he will never return to the round of rebirth. If he is a
Theravadin he will attempt to refute the mahayana path
and he stolidly maintains that the Buddha was merely a
human being.

The four boundless states of mind, or the four stations of
purity, taught by Sakyamuni in his discourses, take a central
place in all Buddhist sadhana, including Tantra. In
Bhandepa's song they are given a mahayana interpretation;
he does not negate the outer, social virtues, but points at the
deeper functions that provoke them. Thus compassion can
degenerate into worthless pity, unless it is inspired by an
insight that involves empathy; sympathetic joy can become
the forced mark of the do-gooder, unless there is an
underlying delight in all perceptual situations; while
equanimity can become the flat response of an anesthetized
mind, rather than awareness of the all-embracing emptiness
that is the common denominator of all experience. Thus to
reconstruct Bhandepa's practice: Through contemplation of
all things as emptiness, and realization of an insubstantial
vision, he attained compassion; through constant
meditation upon that vision with its inherent pleasure, he
attained sympathetic joy; through the resulting activity of
treating all beings like his own sons, with a detachment
arising from meditation on emptiness, he attained loving
kindness; and perceiving all things as a union of space and
awareness, knowing the one taste, he attained his goal of
perfect equanimity.

The Birth of Tujechenpo

The mightiest of all the Bodhisattvas, Chenrezik, his mind intent on the work of saving all beings, took an oath in the presence of the Buddha Amitabha and all the eleven times ten millions of Buddhas, saying, "In me are embodied for work of salvation the deeds and the perfection (which passes human understanding) of all the Buddhas of the three times. I pledge myself to bring every sentient being to the highest and most perfect state of enlightenment. But should I long for rest and peace as to stop in the way, may my head burst into ten pieces as would a cotton ball!"

Then spoke the Buddha Amitabha, "So be it! So be it! This is also the prayer of myself and the Buddhas of the three times inhabiting the ten regions of space. Further, I who am a Buddha will be thy helpmate in the work of saving all creatures!"

Then from out of the body of Chenrezik there came six rays of light which reached the six inhabited worlds. Some rays penetrated to the abodes of the gods where for the purpose of redeeming the gods they became the King of Gods, Indra, and then were heard the sacred words saying, "Subject to the suffering of the fall of the gods through the power of greed and carnal desire, if I have entered the abode of the gods, let there be an end to all the misery of the fall of death and regeneration."

Some rays penetrated to the abode of the fallen gods, asuras, and (as it was with the gods) where for the purpose of redeeming them they became the Lord of the Asuras (Takzangri), and then were heard the sacred words, saying, "Subject to the misery of war through the might of pride and anger, if I have entered the abode of the asuras, let the misery of death and regeneration through the evil of waging war be ended."

And some other rays penetrated to the abode of men, where, for redeeming them they became the Lord of Men, the Mighty One of the Sakyas, Sakyatuba, and then were heard the sacred words saying, "Held in bondage through the power of desire and lust, and subject to the misery of birth, old age, sickness and death, if I have entered the abode of men, let the misery of men be ended."

Some rays penetrated the animal kingdom, where for the purpose of redeeming the animals, they became the Lord of Brute Creation called Great Enduring Lion, Senge Damten, and then were heard the sacred words saying, "Through the power of ignorance, subject to misery of servitude and violent death, if I have entered the abode of the animal kingdom, may all of you now held in the meshes of ignorance, be quickly endowed with enlightenment such as I enjoy."

Some rays entered the abode of the departed, the Pretas, where for the purpose of redeeming them they became the Lord of the Yidaks, Treasury of the sky, Namkhai Dzo, and then were heard the sacred words saying, "Bound through the might of avarice, subject to misery of hunger and thirst, if I have entered the abode of the Yidak, let there be at once an end to hungering and thirsting, and let happiness be reached."

Some rays penetrated the netherworld, where for the purpose of redeeming it they became the lord of the netherworld, King of the Law, Chokigyelpo, and then were heard the sacred words saying, "Bound through the might of lust, subject to the misery of being tormented by heat and cold, if I have truly entered the netherworld, let the torments, the agonies of all beings there be ended."

And then the six classes of sentient beings, who heretofore could not be freed, when arose these six mighty ones from out of the light, and the sacred words were heard, escaped from out of their abodes as out of an iron box which has been opened, and all the six realms were completely emptied of creatures.

Then the Great Compassionate One ascended to the top of Mt Sumeru, and looked with the Eye of Wisdom, and saw that there were as many beings in the world as before, so a second time and a third time in his mercy he emptied the diverse regions of the world, but the numbers of sufferers decreased not, and he was filled with despondence and despair. "Alas!" he cried, "through the instrumentality of the Blessed One innumerable heavenly realms, innumerable regions of sentient beings have been brought into the truth. But though I have released so many beings, yet this orb cannot be emptied even for an instant, and the redemption of the sentient beings is never accomplished! So having found my own peace and happiness I will be with the Completely Passed Away Buddhas." And then he remembered his former prayers, and his head split into a hundred pieces. He cried with pain, which he could not bear, "Alas! merciful Buddhas and Bodhisattvas, and thou Buddha Amitabha, I cry not for myself but out of anguish at not having accomplished the salvation of the world." And he wept aloud.

Then the Buddha Amitabha gathered all the pieces of the head of the Great Compassionate One and made them into eleven faces and as the wheel of transmigration has neither beginning nor end, he made them placid faces, and though placid faces he made them as dark and angry countenances to the wayward man. Moreover he said, "The orb of transmigration has neither beginning nor end, and thou mayest not take beings out of it."

Then spoke the Bodhisattva, "Since I have not been able to remove all beings from the orb of transmigration, may

I have a thousand hands and a thousand eyes so that the thousand hands may be as those of a universal monarch and the thousand eyes as those of the thousand Buddhas of the Bhadrakalpa cycle, and by them I may serve all beings." And at that moment he became endowed with a thousand hands, the palms of his hands in which were a thousand eyes.

Then spoke, Amitabha, the Buddha of Infinite Light, "Most compassionate one, by the following six letters the doors of birth for the six classes of beings may be closed:

OM MA NI PAD ME HŪNG

OM closes the gate of birth among the gods;
MA closes the gate of birth among the asuras;
NI   closes the gate of birth among men;
PAD closes the gate of birth among brute beasts;
ME   closes the gate of birth among the pretas;
HŪNG closes the gate of birth into the netherworld.

These syllables can empty the realms of the six classes of beings. Understand it well, remember them, repeat them and impress them well upon your mind."

Tang Tong Gyelpo's Khakhyapma

In the Buddha, the Dharma and the Bodhisattvas,
we take refuge until our awakening.
Through the merit of our generosity and other selfless
      activity,
may we attain buddha for the sake of all beings.
(*Thrice*).

On the crown of the head,
and upon the heads of all sentient beings everywhere,
on a white lotus and lunar disc, stands the syllable HRĪ
emanating the supreme bodhisattva Chenrezik.
white, radiating a spectrum of rainbow light,
smiling, gazing with compassion in his eyes,
the upper pair of his four arms in namaste-mudra,
the lower pair bears a crystal mala and white lotus.
silks and jewel ornaments arraying his form,
a deerskin mantle about his shoulders,
Amitabha is the centerpiece of his crown,
and his two feet lie in vajra lotus-posture,
while a pellucid moon supports his back.
He is the essence of all places of refuge.

Imagining that all sentient beings are making this
supplication with you in one voice, visualize this:

O Lord,
untainted by any imperfection, pure white in body,
with the perfect buddha ornamenting your crown,
you gaze on all sentient beings with compassion:
We pay homage to you, Chenrezik.

Recite that essential prayer three, seven or as many times
as you are able.

Through this one-pointed supplication
white light radiates from the bodhisattva's body,
cleansing imperfect action, vision and confused perception,
and through Chenrezik's empowering body, speech and mind,
the outer chalice is transformed into buddhafields of bliss,
and the inner elixir, the body, speech and mind of all beings,
into empty light-form, sound and awareness.

Visualize that process as you recite the above lines and then
chant this mantra:

OM MANI PADME HŪNG HRI

Repeat the mantra until you attain some success.
Finally, keep the wheels of body, speech and mind
composed in basic space free of thought.

One's own and others' bodies and all appearances are the
      Bodhisattva's Body;
All sound whatsoever is the harmony of the six-syllable
      mantra;
And all thought is a vast space of magnificent awareness.

Through the merit of this practice
Quickly accomplishing Chenrezik,
May all beings without a single exception
Reach his paradise.

The Bodhisattva's Thirty-Seven Observances

To restate the ambience in which these mahayana texts are expedient, primarily we may simply revel in the joy of the sentiment and the form, in the bodhisattvic morality and the poetry, in which case the relativity, the implied gradualism of the Mahayana is inseparable from nondual Dzogchen awareness. And secondly, when the density of karmic dependence has become impenetrable, when knots in the nadis have become stubbornly resistant, this manifestation of great compassion for self and other can revert to nondual transcendence.

We can never lose identity with the nature of mind once it has been revealed in initiatory experience, and it is that view of the totality that allows us access to the entire spectrum of skilful means, including the repertoire of mahayana and hinayana Buddhism, of deistic religion and of psychotherapy and shamanism. Here we invoke Avalokiteshwara, Avalokita, Lokeshwara, a sambhogakaya emanation of light-form representing totality – ultimate compassion manifest in spacetime – to provide a haven for the embodied bodhisattva.

The bodhisattva's refuge assumed, activity flows naturally, effortlessly, in concert with Avalokita, and here the nature of that activity is displayed as compassion manifest. It is not a discipline to impose upon a reluctant body/mind; it is the manner in which bodhichitta shows itself in the face of human suffering. We acknowledge this dimension of pure being when our empathetic compassion is caught in a relativistic trap. When karma leaves us there we need to be able to recognize our inevitable response.

This eight-hundred-year-old Tibetan scripture provides a
nonsectarian invocation.

NAMO LOKESWARAYA!

To Avalokita, to the supreme guru
abiding in the stillness of every situation,
alive solely for the sake of others
I pay constant homage with devoted body, speech and
  mind.

The perfect buddhas, founts of blessings,
arose from mastery of the sacred lore:
since buddhahood depends upon knowledge of the
  practice
here is an explanation of the bodhisattva's observances.

1.
Now, finally endowed with this precious human body,
a boat to carry us across the ocean of confusion,
the bodhisattva listens, reflects and meditates,
unceasingly, through day and night.

2.
With attachment to friends rolling like the ocean,
with hatred towards enemies burning like wildfire,
in the murk of undiscriminating torpor
the bodhisattva leaves his homeland.

3.
Avoiding provocative situations, nervousness decreases,
free from agitation, contentment increases,
and clear knowledge begets confidence on the path:
the bodhisattva, therefore, seeks seclusion.

4.
Relations and friends of a lifetime must part,
hard won wealth must be left behind at last,

consciousness forsakes the body like a guest a hotel:
the bodhisattva, therefore, forsakes concern for this life.

5.

Keeping company with others excites the three poisons
and impairs study, reflection and meditation:
the bodhisattva shuns misleading companions
who reject loving kindness and compassion.

6.

Through devoted service frustration ends
and excellence increases like the waxing moon:
the bodhisattva cherishes his spiritual friend
more than his own body.

7.

Still chained in the prison of samsara,
can the gods of this world protect us?
the bodhisattva takes refuge in the Three Jewels,
which provide unfailing and undeceiving protection.

8.

The Buddha foretold that the result of misdoing
is insufferable pain in the lower realms:
the bodhisattva avoids such error
even at the cost of his own life.

9.

Sensual, aesthetic or intellectual pleasure,
like the morning dew, lasts only a moment:
the bodhisattva aspires to the Unchangeable,
the highest level of liberation.

10.

Blessed with her affection from beginningless time,
how can we be happy while our mother suffers?
In order to liberate all beings of the universe
the bodhisattva fosters bodhichitta.

11.
All suffering arises out of selfish desire;
perfect-buddha springs from a charitable mind:
the bodhisattva exchanges his happiness
for the suffering of others.

12.
To the thief in the throes of avarice
conniving and stealing another's possessions,
the bodhisattva devotes his charity,
his body, his substance and his time.

13.
When someone attempts to harm him,
although he is innocent and faultless,
the bodhisattva, out of compassion,
takes the malefactor's sins upon himself.

14.
For whoever reviles and abuses him
and publicly slanders him,
the bodhisattva bestows nothing but praise
and loving kindness.

15.
To whoever provokes, exposes and shames him,
singling him out among many for derision,
conceiving that tormentor as a spiritual friend
the bodhisattva bows low in devotion.

16.
To him whom he cherishes as a son
and who regards him with enmity in return,
the bodhisattva increases affection,
like a mother to her plague-stricken child.

17.
When his equals or inferiors in their conceit
find occasion to treat him with contempt,
with the same devotion he shows his gurus
the bodhisattva esteems and honors them.

18.
When poverty-stricken and despised,
outcaste and plagued by disease and demons,
the bodhisattva remains undaunted,
absorbing universal sin and suffering.

19.
Flattered by the multitude and revered,
as wealthy as divine Kubera himself,
yet seeing the meaningless vanity of existence
the bodhisattva is free of pride.

20.
If rage, an enemy within, is not beaten,
formidable enemies proliferate outside:
with the armies of loving kindness and compassion
the bodhisattva subdues his own mind.

21.
Coveted possessions are like draughts of salt water—
the more we have, the more we want:
the bodhisattva instinctively relinquishes
the things that breed compulsive desire.

22.
All forms of appearance are mind
and mind in itself is essentially empty:
knowing such truth, the bodhisattva
accepts the frangibility of both self and other.

23.
In his encounter with things attractive,
regarding them as unreal, as mere beautiful light,
the bodhisattva relinquishes compulsive desires
as lightly as summer rainbows.

24.
All suffering is like the dream-death of an only son,
and reifying delusive appearances is sickening:
when the bodhisattva encounters repulsion
he treats it like delusory dream.

25.
If even the body can be sacrificed for buddha,
what need be said of material things?
Without hope for return or reward
the bodhisattva donates alms.

26.
Without discipline we cannot help ourselves
and to impose oneself upon others is futile:
the bodhisattva maintains a moral discipline
that is free from temporal hankering.

27.
The buddha-son who longs for ultimate happiness
treats adventure in temptation as a gold mine:
the bodhisattva maintains meditative patience,
constantly, devoid of any ill will.

28.
Even self-seeking Disciples and Hermits
can turn back the fire that runs to the head:
the bodhisattva arouses persistent energy
only as power to act for others.

29.

With insight that is intrinsically still,
pure perception destroys emotivity:
the bodhisattva observes meditative absorption
that transcends the four formless states.

30.

If the five perfections lack penetrating insight
perfect enlightenment is relinquished:
in the skilful bodhisattva with that insight
actor, action and acted upon are one.

31.

Without scrutiny of the confused mind
any outward piety is hypocrisy:
the bodhisattva employs exploring intelligence
to destroy underlying bewilderment.

32.

Dwelling on the faults of other buddha-sons
we corrupt ourselves:
the bodhisattva refrains from relating the failures
of brothers and sisters in the Mahayana.

33.

Disputing with others for profit or respect
impairs study, reflection and meditation:
in the houses of his friends and patrons
the bodhisattva relinquishes self-interest.

34.

Harsh words disturb other people's minds
and the bodhisattva's career is impaired:
we avoid abusive talk
distasteful in other's ears.

35.
It is difficult to reverse emotional habits,
but alert and mindful, applying antidotes,
the bodhisattva allays uprising passion,
quelling lust, anger or jealousy as it appears.

36.
In short, in all interaction with others,
conscious of mind's passing show,
maintaining presence, with constant attention
the bodhisattva strives for the good of others.

37.
The merit that is won by living like that,
invested in the suffering of all beings,
penetrating insight purifying giver, gift and recipient,
the bodhisattva shares his enlightenment.

Following my guru's instructions,
inspired by sutras, tantras and shastras,
for bodhisattva-aspirants I have composed
'The Bodhisattva's Thirty-seven Observances'.

My intellect may be weak and my training poor,
and my poetry may not please the critics,
but based on the sutras and my guru's precepts
I pray that these Observances may be free from error.

The subtleties of bodhisattvic activity
are hard to fathom for a person like me:

I crave the guru's indulgence
for contradictions and any flaws.

Through the merit of this work
may all beings attain Lord Avalokita
free from the extremes of samsara and nirvana,
ultimatete and relative.

Sarva Mangalam!

Christian Love and Charity

Can we treat Christian 'charity' as a synonym of Dzogchen compassion? In New Testament poetry, charity seems to imply precisely what we mean by great compassion in Dzogchen. In this excerpt from the King James Bible, I Corinthians 13:1-7, I was tempted to replace 'charity' by 'compassion' (tujé in Tibetan or karuna *in Sanskrit), but rejected the notion because it does the Shakespearian language no good.*

However, before we can accept this divine poetry as Dzogchen, we must understand that compassion/charity is innate, the underlying, stable state of mind, and that although poetically we may cry histrionically that we do not have it, through initiatory experience of the nature of mind we know that compassion/charity is intrinsically present, always there for its bare recognition and acceptance.

Further, does this Christian charity not wear the mask of humility and self-sacrifice? Yes, and that is surely enough good, but doesn't the All-Good Kuntuzangpo/ Samantabhadra overtake the Good of Jesus, the Lamb of God? Probably not – we must remember that the Gospels were written and compiled largely by children for children but in their exoteric simplicity they are no less meaningful for that.

"Though I speak with the tongues of men and of angels, and have not charity, I am become as sounding brass, or a tinkling cymbal. And though I have the gift of prophecy, and understand all mysteries, and all knowledge; and though I have all faith, so that I could remove mountains, and have not charity, I am nothing. And though I bestow all my goods to feed the poor, and though I give my body to be burned, and have not charity, it profiteth me nothing.

Charity suffereth long, and is kind; charity envieth not; charity vaunteth not itself, is not puffed up, doth not behave itself unseemly, seeketh not her own, is not easily provoked, thinketh no evil; rejoiceth not in iniquity, but rejoiceth in the truth; beareth all things, believeth all things, hopeth all things, endureth all things."

These next verses, I Corinthians 13:11-13, imply that knowledge of charity/compassion is dependent upon initiatory experience of the nature of mind, and, to mix metaphors, until we have bathed in 'the blood of the lamb' we are stranded in 'the confusion of samsara'.

[11] "When I was a child, I spake as a child, I understood as a child, I thought as a child; but when I became a man, I put away childish things. [12]For now we see through a glass, darkly; but then surely face to face. Now I know in part, but then I shall know even as also I am known. [13]And now abideth faith, hope and charity, these three; but the greatest of these is love."

The Twenty-Seven Moral Indications

*Once we have opened ourselves to the nature of mind it
provides spontaneously whatever the universe and its
sentient beings require to sustain the perfection of the
moment. When karma grabs us by the short and curlies,
leaving us in samsaric confusion, the bodhisattva's twenty-
seven exoteric indications of appropriate activity clears
the way for a return to the clarity of initiatory experience.
A word of warning: if these indications are taken as 'vows'
then inevitably conflict will arise with the bodhisattva's
imperative to do whatsoever benefits all sentient beings
and the Dzogchen imperative of spontaneity. While these
outer vows of body, speech and mind are the imperative
vows for gradual-path applicants, any mindless adherence
to moral principle becomes an obstacle to fulfilment of the
imperative Dzogchen spontaneity.*

Vows of Body
Outer
To refrain from killing.
To refrain from sexual activity (or sexual misconduct).
To refrain from stealing.

Inner
To refrain from self-abuse.
To refrain from holding vajra-relatives in contempt.
To refrain from misusing dharma symbols.

Secret
To refrain from stepping even on the shadow of the
        lama; (to act conscientiously in his presence).
To refrain from harassing (making sexual advances
        to) the lama's consort or vajra-brothers' consorts.
To refrain from striking one's vajra-brothers or sisters.

Vows of Speech
Outer
To refrain from lying.
To refrain from divisive speech (slander).
To refrain from harsh speech.

Inner
To refrain from verbal disrespect to teachers.
To refrain from disrespect to those who ponder the dharma.
To refrain from disrespect to those who are meditating on
    the absolute.

Secret
To refrain from deriding the lama's consort.
To refrain from deriding one's vajra brothers or sisters.
To refrain from deriding one's teacher.

[Also: To refrain from disrespect to the speech of the vajra
family; to refrain from speaking negatively about the
conduct of the lama; to disregard the lama's advice.]

Vows of Mind
Outer
To refrain from covetousness (craving).
To refrain from malice (ill will).
To refrain from wrong views.

Inner
To refrain from perverted (nonconscientious) activities.
To refrain from excitation and torpor in meditation.
To refrain from perverted views (eternalism, nihilism, etc.).

Secret
To visualize the lama and dakini (within every 24 hours).
To perform guru-yoga or visualize the yidam (every 24
    hours).
To rehearse Dzogchen view, meditation and action (every
    24 hours).

Acknowledgements

The Prayer of the Three Yogas
This prayer, taken from the *Kama*, translated by Tulku
 Padma Wongyel and Kunzang Tenzin (Keith Dowman) in
 1969 has been thoroughly amended in 2021.

*Yeshe Tsogyel and the Seven Thieves and Yeshe Tsogyel's
 Song of the Four Joys.*
Taken from Sky *Dancer*, trans. Keith Dowman, SUNY,
 1981, pp.45 & 118.

Dzogchen Vimalakirti Nirdesha Sutra
Thanks to Robert Thurman for the immaculate basic
translation (available online) of the 9th chapter of Licchabi
Vimalakirti's sutra from the Sanskrit, amended to reflect a
Dzogchen rendition of the classical sutra.

The Siddha Bhandepa
 Taken from *Masters of Mahamudra*, trans. Keith Dowman,
 SUNY, 1985 p.191-4.

The Birth of Tujechenpo
 Anonymous.

Tangtong Gyelpo's Khakhyapma
The mahasiddha Tangtong Gyelpo's quintessential altruistic
 recitation and visualization of Tujechenpo's *Khakhyapma*.

Bodhisattva's Thirty-Seven Observances
"This work was composed by the teacher of scripture and
 language Tokme Zangpo (1245-1369) in the Precious
 Quicksilver Cave for the sake of all beings."
It was taught as preliminary instruction to the
 Kalachakra Tantra initiation given in Bodhagaya by the
 Dalai Lama Tenzin Gyatso in March 1974. It has been
 translated by Kunzang Tenzin, during the summer of
 1974 in Kathmandu.

Dzogchen Teaching Series

Radical Dzogchen: Available on Amazon

Nonmeditation
Daily Practice
Semdzins
Dzogchen View
SAMAYA
Khorde Rushen
BUSUKU
Lama and Lineage
Pilgrimage
Mahamudra
Bardo
Compassion
Sex